Ted Harrison

Children of the Yukon

SO-CFF-839

To Huron County Library & all it members. Fond regards from Ted Harrison 78

Date Due

Dec 14 '78			
De 23 '78	Jan 2/8		
Ja 11 79			
Ja 20 79	fOR Dec 91		
Fe 3 7 9	Jan 2/92		
VAN Dec 8 5	UL 3 1 199		
Crediton			

Tundra Books

Winter and night come early to the Yukon. In November, by mid-afternoon darkness has already fallen on Dawson City and its ghost buildings. Children make snowmen on their way home from school; soon the intense dry cold will make the snow too powdery for packing.

The Yukon as I found it

It was a cloudless summer day in 1968 when I arrived in the village of Carcross in the Yukon where I had been hired to teach school. I had traveled widely in the world and even taught in a few beautiful and exotic places, but as I stood on the edge of Bennett Lake that day and stared across to the snowcapped mountains that rose from the other edge, I turned to my wife and said: "This is Shangri-la." Not a very original observation perhaps, but it did express my feelings at having come across a secret world of incredible beauty and peace.

In the nine years since then, I have visited most of the settlements in the Yukon, traveled on many of its long rivers and huge lakes and even seen some of its wilderness – the absolute wildness of the forest near Carcross was another strong first impression. But I feel I have only begun to know it. How quickly can one get to know a land bigger than Spain? It is easier to know the people. There are only 23,000 and they are very friendly.

What I have painted in this book are scenes that have impressed me. It is not a complete picture. Children in the towns of the Yukon do many things other North American children do: they go to school, watch TV, play basketball in winter and baseball in summer. But they also do things children further south never have a chance to do, and this is what I have painted. Not how the Yukon is the same, but how it differs.

Looking back, I am glad I arrived in summer or I might not have been so favorably impressed. That first winter the temperature dropped to 50 degrees below zero Fahrenheit and stayed there *for a whole month!* How could anything be so cold? That was when I first really noticed the ravens. The streets were deserted except for those amazing black creatures as numerous and noisy and lively as ever.

One other aspect of nature impressed me more in the Yukon than elsewhere – the skies. They are big and there is always something different going on in them: northern lights, midnight suns, strange-colored moons, stars that look handset in the night sky, spectacular dawns and sunsets. Even simple things surprise, like the way smoke rises straight upward on a very cold winter's day. And the surprises never stop.

Ted Harrison
June 1977
Whitehorse, Yukon, Canada

On Bonanza Creek where the first Klondike gold discovery was made, today only a few people – children,
placer miners, tourists – pan for gold. Behind them
amid large mounds of washed-out gravel, a huge
dredge stands abandoned. It once worked twenty-four
hours a day sifting the creek bed for gold.

The gold rush and history

Although the Yukon has ghost towns, ghost cabins, ghost paddlewheelers, and even a ghost church that one can explore in summer and relive the famous Klondike gold rush, I think of it most often in winter. For then I am most conscious of what those poor dreamers went through.

It all started on a fine day in August, 1896, when three Yukoners, out for the day from a fishing camp, found gold in the bed of Rabbit Creek. George Carmack, Skookum Jim and Tagish Charlie staked their claim and rushed to the mining commissioner's office at Forty Mile to register it. Word spread at an amazing speed for those days. Within a year all the world knew of the gold strike in the Yukon. The name of the creek was changed to Bonanza; Dawson City sprang up to become the center of world attention. The fantastic stampede for gold began.

Nobody took exact statistics, but it is said that out of 100,000 men who left homes in 50 countries around the world to come to the Klondike, only 40,000 made it. Many turned back when they ran out of supplies and realized what the Yukon winter meant. Some starved or froze to death. None expected the disappointment of ending up empty handed after so much effort. There was gold in the Klondike, but it wasn't for the newcomers. Veteran miners of the area had staked all the best ground. In 1898, Dawson City boasted 25,000 citizens; by 1905 half had left. Today it is a ghost town just rebuilding with many reminders of that brief heyday when women walked the streets in the latest Paris fashions, gold dust was weighed as money, and honky-tonk piano filled the night with revelry.

The last gold dredges in the Yukon stopped working in 1966. When I visited Bonanza Creek a few years later I watched my young son and friends do what thousands had done before them: sift a tray of gravel from the riverbed – just on a chance.

The story of the gold rush period has been preserved in many vivid accounts, including one of the most popular narrative poems in the English language: Robert Service's "The Cremation of Sam McGee." It begins:

There are strange things done in the midnight sun
By the men who moil for gold;
The Arctic trails have their secret tales
That would make your blood run cold;
The Northern Lights have seen queer sights,
But the queerest they ever did see
Was that night on the marge of Lake Lebarge...

Discovery was a booming camp in northern British Columbia during the gold rush days. Today it is a ghost town (near Atlin, B.C.) where children explore abandoned miners' shacks, hotels and empty saloons.

Every August 17th, children – and parents – come from all over the Yukon to Dawson City where they dress up in the styles of the Gay 90s and celebrate the day gold was found back in 1896. Parades, raft racing, baseball and a show in the old Palace Grand Theater are part of Discovery Day fun.

As regular as winter, the ravens return to the towns and villages of the Yukon from their summer nesting places. Noisy, bold and black against the snow, they make no concession to the silence and the changing color of the land, but scatter garbage, tease dogs and fight over food thrown to them by the children.

On Nares Lake at Carcross, children play, haul water from ice holes and frolic around the *S.S. Tutshi*, a retired paddlewheeler that still watches over the village from its resting place on shore. It was one of many sternwheelers that supplied northern communities in summer carrying passengers and freight, before roads were built.

The sound of dogs barking and children laughing often means a snowshoe race is in progress. Running on snowshoes is difficult but fun. Even beginners laugh at themselves as they trip and tumble, and struggle to get back upright.

In February, mushers from all over the North bring their teams of trained huskies to Whitehorse for the "Yukon Sourdough Rendezvous." The 45-mile race on the frozen Yukon River is a memorial to the days before roads and planes when the dogsled and horse-drawn sleighs were the only winter transportation. Children cheer from the sidelines.

Fishing as well as trapping goes on in winter. Boys help fathers fish through the ice on Crag Lake near Carcross.

The snowshoe rabbit is snared for food and fur – to make mukluks and mittens. A unique rabbit with large furry feet that help it hop on snow, it changes its coat from brown in summer to white in winter.

"Have you got your moose?" is a common greeting during the hunting season, for the lordly moose still provides much meat for food, leather for clothing and antlers for carving. Successful hunters carry their trophy home proudly, for the hunt has usually been a hard one over rough wilderness and muskeg.

Tauk ee tee see go in the Tlingit language means "Joyous Summer Day Festival." It is held each year at Tagish by the native people from all around the area (Whitehorse, Tagish and Carcross) with dancing and singing around a blazing campfire. Broiled moose meat and fish are served.

Summer and Indians

All children of the Yukon do many of the same things, particularly in summer when the days are long. They get up very early and go to bed late, boat and canoe, fish, camp, pick berries and just generally enjoy the wilderness. And yet there are native communities in the Yukon where life is different from that in other towns. In summer, many Indian families move out to fishing camps and set up drying racks along the river-banks. Dog-salmon and king-salmon are caught on the Yukon River and smoked in the traditional way.

The native people who live in the Yukon are Athabas-cans, one of the most widely scattered groups of In-dians in North America. They include the Navajo and Apache in the United States, the Beaver and Carrier in British Columbia, the Tutchone of the southern Yukon and the Old Crow (or Loucheux) of the northern Yukon. For thousands of years they have been hunters and gatherers, traveling over large areas in search of food. At Old Crow inside the Arctic Circle, I felt the continuity of history in people rather than books.

Today the Indians struggle to preserve their traditional way of life against the insatiable hunger of the south for oil and minerals. Town dwellers try to adapt the best of life in the south to the demands of the North. One question kept occurring to me when I was paint-ing the children in this book:

"Will these children of today's Yukon be permitted to decide its future, or will it be done for them by others – far away in boardrooms and government offices – who may never even have seen this remarkable land?"

At Ross River the native people smoke moosehides by making teepees of them and building a fire inside. A well-cured moosehide has a wonderful smoked smell and makes warm tough clothing and footwear. Beads are sewn in beautiful patterns on these handicraft items.

The northernmost settlement in the Yukon is Old Crow, an Indian village above the Arctic Circle. Summer is the signal for everyone to go fishing and muskrat trapping, while the midnight sun casts its orange glow over the land. In autumn the children also take part in the caribou hunt, a big event of the year. The old village bell announced emergencies.

Fire, not cold, is the dread of the North. Unlike the magnificent skies admired for the northern lights, midnight suns, great dawns and sunsets, a sky lit by a distant forest fire holds only terror for the watchers. To enter an area recently destroyed by fire is an awesome and saddening experience.

Before modern fire equipment arrived, everyone – children, too – turned out to help work the old Carcross fire pumper. It fought so many cabin fires and was so loved that when it was finally retired, it refused to leave the area, breaking down near Rainbow Lake on the way to Whitehorse.

In the Yukon every family seems to own a canoe or boat. As soon as the last ice leaves the lakes and rivers, there is a great rush toward the water – as if everyone is desperate to enjoy the long days of the brief summer. Rivers were once the only means of access to many communities; now there are roads everywhere except to Old Crow.

Near Carcross is the smallest desert in the world, and in spring it becomes an unusual racetrack as children ride bareback over the sand dunes. The packhorses, so useful for big game hunts in the mountain terrain, seem to enjoy the game as much as the youngsters.

Religion has many faces in the North. In native cemeteries, small houses were built over graves and a favorite possession was laid inside, such as a toy for a dead child.

Sunday, outside the churches, there is nearly always a dog which has followed his young master there and been left at the door.

On a hill at Bennett, B.C., the old Presbyterian Church looks down on children exploring for relics of the gold rush. Built to welcome the miners who had struggled on foot across the dangerous Chilkoot Pass in '98, it was left unused when the rush to the Klondike ended. In the distance, the train from Skagway, Alaska to Whitehorse passes through some of the most beautiful mountains in North America.

Ted Harrison

Since coming to live and teach in the Yukon in 1968, Ted Harrison has become its best-known painter. A series of one-man art exhibitions in Vancouver, Toronto, Ottawa, Montreal and Edmonton have made him as popular in the cities of southern Canada as in the North, where he has exhibited not only in the Yukon but also in Alaska.

He taught school in Malaya and New Zealand, as well as in his native England where he graduated from the West Hartlepool College of Art and the University of Durham in Newcastle-upon-Tyne. He and his Scottish-born wife and son came to Canada in 1967. While teaching on the Wabasca Indian Reserve in northern Alberta, he wrote and illustrated a book for his pupils called *Northland Alphabet,* using subjects native to the area. He and his family now live in Whitehorse where he teaches art at F. H. Collins High School. Summers and weekends he spends in his cabin near Carcross, painting and fishing.

This book is dedicated to his wife, Nicky, and their son, Charles.

The Yukon

The Yukon covers an area of 207, 076 square miles in the northwest corner of Canada, east of Alaska. Its population of 23,000 includes 5,000 school-age children. Statistics on the native Indian population vary (depending on who is doing the counting) from 2,580 to 6,000. The capital city of Whitehorse has a population of 15,300 and is the transportation hub and supply center. The St. Elias mountain range is the highest in Canada, and Mt. Logan is the highest peak, 19,850 feet. In winter the average daily temperature is $-18°C$ or zero F; in summer it is $10°C$ ($55°F$). Major industries are mining (silver, coal, lead, tungsten, copper, zinc and asbestos); tourism; fur trapping (muskrat, mink, marten, beaver, fox and squirrel) and big game hunting.

The Yukon became a Territory of Canada in 1898 by Act of Parliament. It is administered by a local government of 12 elected members of the Legislative Assembly headed by a Commissioner appointed by the Minister of Indian Affairs and Northern Development for the Government of Canada. The Territory is represented in the Canadian House of Commons in Ottawa by one elected member.

©1977, Ted Harrison
Published in Canada by Tundra Books of Montreal, Montreal, Quebec   H3G 1J6
ISBN 0-88776-092-9
Published in the United States by Tundra Books of Northern New York, Plattsburgh, N.Y. 12901
ISBN 0-912766-83-2   Library of Congress Card No. 77-79543
Design by Rolf Harder, Design Collaborative, Montreal
Printed in Canada by Pierre Des Marais Inc., Montreal
Excerpt from "The Cremation of Sam McGee" from *The Collected Poems of Robert Service*
Reprinted by permission of
McGraw-Hill Ryerson Limited, Toronto, and Dodd, Mead & Co., New York.

The paintings in this book were given a special exhibition at the Shayne Gallery, Montreal.